Bear's ABC Book

ABC

The ABCs of Social & Emotional Learning

Written & Illustrated by Lindsey Kealey

PAWsitive Choices®

This book is lovingly dedicated to the amazing young learners, who are my teachers.

Kealey, Lindsey-author, illustrator
Bear's ABC Book/Lindsey Kealey

ISBN 978-1-7357367-5-4

Published by PAWsitive Choices, LLC
Bend, OR, USA

What is PAWsitive Choices?

PAWsitive Choices Social & Emotional Learning is an easy-to-use guide for teachers and families that teaches social and emotional learning skills through engaging stories. Research-based strategies are interwoven throughout the curriculum to support optimal brain development and help children thrive.

PAWsitive Choices teaches you how to:

- Solve problems
- Learn from mistakes
- Set goals
- Make positive choices
- Talk about feelings
- Listen and think
- Make healthy choices
- Take brain breaks
- Take calming breaths
- Use positive self-talk

Visit pawsitivechoices.com to learn more.

A Note to Grown-Ups: Literacy Skills

Literacy in early childhood lays the foundation for children's development of reading and writing skills. This book focuses on the important literacy skill of **alphabet knowledge**. This includes:

- Understanding how words are used (in books, on street signs, etc.)
- Identifying letters of the alphabet (uppercase and lowercase)
- Producing the correct sound associated with letters

Source: Oregon's Early Learning & Kindergarten Guidelines

A Note to Grown-Ups: Social & Emotional Skills

Each page in this book teaches a **social and emotional learning** (SEL) skill. SEL is important for helping children make positive choices, regulate emotions, solve problems, and develop healthy relationships. Some benefits of SEL include:

- Improvement in relationships and self-concept
- Increased academic performance
- Decline in students' behavior problems & anxiety

Source: Collaborative for Academic, Social & Emotional Learning (2021)

Scan the QR codes throughout the book for fun kid-friendly videos.

Aa

Ask for help.

B b
Take a brain break.

Cc

Take calming breaths.

D d
Follow directions.

Ee

Enjoy time with others.

F f

Share your feelings.

Gg

Set goals.

Hh

Make healthy choices.

I i

Use ignore power.

Jj

Ask others to join you.

Kk

Be kind.

Ll

Listen and think.

What do you like to do?

Mm
Make positive choices.

Nn

Say, "No, thank you."

Oo

Stay on task.

Pp

Solve problems.

Qq

When do you use a
quiet voice?

Rr

Be responsible.

S s

Be safe.

T t
Take turns.

Uu

Put your hand up.

Vv

Visualize your happy place.

W w

Walk away.

Xx

Exercise.

Yy

Your brain is amazing!

Zz

zoom helps us learn.

About the Author

Lindsey Kealey is a university instructor of education, speaker, coach, and creator of PAWsitive Choices Social and Emotional Learning. She earned a Bachelor of Science in Human Development and Family Sciences with an emphasis in child development and holds a Master of Arts in Teaching. Her university work, as well as her experience teaching in public schools, helped her craft a trauma-informed curriculum that integrates neuroscience, social and emotional learning, and problem solving into a program that helps children thrive. A California native, she now lives in Central Oregon and enjoys exploring the outdoors with her family and pug.

For more information about PAWsitive Choices curriculum, trainings, and events, visit www.pawsitivechoices.com or send an email to info@pawsitivechoices.com. Check out The PAWsitive Choices Podcast to learn more about topics in social and emotional learning.

Visit our website for more curriculum!

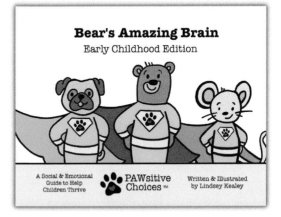

Check out our other products on Amazon!